EMMANUEL JOSEPH

Beyond Maps, how Politics, Culture, and Business Redefine Global Progress

Copyright © 2025 by Emmanuel Joseph

All rights reserved. No part of this publication may be reproduced, stored or transmitted in any form or by any means, electronic, mechanical, photocopying, recording, scanning, or otherwise without written permission from the publisher. It is illegal to copy this book, post it to a website, or distribute it by any other means without permission.

First edition

This book was professionally typeset on Reedsy. Find out more at reedsy.com

Contents

1 Chapter 1   1
2 Chapter 13: The Role of Education in Global Progress   16

1

Chapter 1

Chapter 1: The Intersection of Politics and Culture Politics and culture have always been intertwined, each influencing the other in profound ways. As political systems evolve, they shape the cultural norms and values of societies, fostering either inclusivity or division. For instance, democratic governance tends to promote cultural diversity and the free exchange of ideas, while authoritarian regimes may suppress cultural expressions that challenge their authority. The complex dance between politics and culture is a dynamic force that drives societal change and progress.

One of the most striking examples of this interplay is seen in the realm of human rights. Political movements advocating for civil liberties and equality have often emerged from cultural shifts in public consciousness. The civil rights movement in the United States, for instance, was deeply rooted in cultural expressions of resistance and solidarity, from protest songs to influential literature. Such movements not only change political landscapes but also redefine cultural identities.

Moreover, the globalization of culture has led to the diffusion of political ideas across borders. The spread of democratic values, for instance, has been facilitated by the global reach of media and the internet. People in different parts of the world are exposed to diverse cultural narratives that challenge their existing political beliefs and inspire new forms of activism.

This cultural exchange fosters a global sense of interconnectedness and shared responsibility.

In recent years, the rise of social media has amplified the cultural impact on politics. Platforms like Twitter and Facebook have become powerful tools for political mobilization and cultural expression. They enable individuals and groups to connect, share their experiences, and organize movements that transcend national boundaries. This digital revolution has democratized the way politics and culture interact, making it easier for marginalized voices to be heard and for global solidarity to be forged.

Chapter 2: Economic Globalization and Cultural Identity The forces of economic globalization have had a profound impact on cultural identities around the world. As businesses expand across borders and markets become interconnected, local cultures are both challenged and enriched by global influences. This process of cultural exchange can lead to the erosion of traditional practices, but it also creates opportunities for cultural revival and innovation.

In many cases, economic globalization has resulted in the homogenization of cultures. The spread of multinational corporations and consumer products has introduced standardized lifestyles and values to diverse societies. Fast food chains, fashion brands, and entertainment conglomerates promote a global culture that often overshadows local traditions. This can lead to the loss of cultural heritage and the displacement of indigenous practices.

However, economic globalization also fosters cultural hybridization. As people from different cultural backgrounds interact through trade, tourism, and migration, they exchange ideas and create new cultural forms. For example, fusion cuisine combines elements from various culinary traditions, reflecting the blending of cultures in globalized cities. Similarly, music genres like hip-hop and electronic dance music incorporate influences from around the world, creating a vibrant global cultural landscape.

Furthermore, economic globalization has empowered local cultures to assert their identities on the global stage. Many communities have leveraged global markets to promote their cultural products, from handicrafts to traditional performances. This not only preserves cultural heritage but also generates economic opportunities for artisans and performers. The rise of cultural tourism, for instance, allows travelers to experience and appreciate the richness of local cultures, while supporting the livelihoods of local communities.

Ultimately, economic globalization and cultural identity are inextricably linked. While globalization can pose challenges to cultural preservation, it also offers opportunities for cultural expression and innovation. By embracing the complexities of this relationship, societies can navigate the tensions between global integration and local identity, fostering a more inclusive and diverse world.

Chapter 3: The Role of Business in Social Progress Businesses play a crucial role in driving social progress, as they have the resources, influence, and reach to effect significant change. By adopting socially responsible practices, companies can contribute to the well-being of their employees, communities, and the environment. This chapter explores how businesses can be agents of positive change and the challenges they face in balancing profit with social impact.

Corporate social responsibility (CSR) has become a key focus for many businesses, as they recognize the importance of aligning their operations with ethical and sustainable principles. Through CSR initiatives, companies can address social issues such as poverty, inequality, and environmental degradation. For example, many companies invest in education and healthcare programs for underserved communities, improving the quality of life for countless individuals. Additionally, businesses can adopt sustainable practices that reduce their environmental footprint, contributing to the fight against climate change.

Another way businesses drive social progress is through inclusive hiring and workplace diversity. By creating diverse and inclusive work environments, companies can tap into a broader range of perspectives and talents, fostering innovation and creativity. This not only enhances their competitiveness but also promotes social cohesion and equality. Companies that prioritize diversity and inclusion send a powerful message about the value of different backgrounds and experiences, challenging societal norms and reducing discrimination.

However, businesses also face challenges in balancing profit with social impact. The pursuit of profit can sometimes lead to unethical practices, such as labor exploitation and environmental harm. To mitigate these risks, businesses must establish strong ethical frameworks and accountability mechanisms. This includes transparent reporting, stakeholder engagement, and adherence to international standards. By integrating ethical considerations into their core operations, companies can build trust with their stakeholders and contribute to long-term social progress.

Ultimately, the role of business in social progress is multifaceted and evolving. Companies have the potential to be powerful agents of change, but they must navigate complex ethical dilemmas and stakeholder expectations. By embracing their social responsibilities, businesses can contribute to a more equitable and sustainable future, where economic success goes hand in hand with social well-being.

Chapter 4: The Impact of Political Decisions on Global Business
Political decisions have far-reaching implications for global business, as they shape the regulatory and economic environment in which companies operate. From trade policies to environmental regulations, political choices can either facilitate or hinder business activities. This chapter examines how political decisions impact global business and the strategies companies employ to navigate these challenges.

Trade policies are one of the most significant political factors affecting global business. Tariffs, trade agreements, and import/export restrictions can influence market access and competitiveness. For example, the implementation of trade tariffs can increase the cost of goods, making it difficult for businesses to compete in foreign markets. Conversely, free trade agreements can open new opportunities for businesses by reducing barriers and creating a level playing field. Companies must closely monitor trade policies and adapt their strategies to mitigate risks and capitalize on opportunities.

Environmental regulations are another key area where political decisions impact global business. Governments around the world are increasingly implementing regulations to address climate change and environmental degradation. These regulations can affect business operations, requiring companies to adopt sustainable practices and invest in green technologies. While compliance with environmental regulations can be costly, it also presents opportunities for innovation and differentiation. Businesses that lead in sustainability can enhance their brand reputation and gain a competitive edge in the market.

Political instability and geopolitical tensions also pose challenges for global business. Conflicts, sanctions, and political unrest can disrupt supply chains, create uncertainty, and increase operational risks. Companies operating in politically volatile regions must develop robust risk management strategies to ensure business continuity. This includes diversifying supply chains, establishing contingency plans, and engaging with local stakeholders to navigate complex political landscapes. By proactively addressing political risks, businesses can safeguard their operations and maintain resilience in the face of uncertainty.

In addition to navigating political decisions, businesses also have the power to influence political outcomes. Through advocacy and lobbying, companies can shape public policy and contribute to the development of a favorable business environment. However, this influence must be exercised responsibly, with a focus on ethical considerations and the public good. By engaging in transparent and accountable advocacy, businesses can contribute to positive political and economic outcomes that benefit society as a whole.

Chapter 5: Cultural Diplomacy and International Relations Cultural diplomacy plays a vital role in fostering international relations and promoting mutual understanding between nations. By leveraging cultural exchange and collaboration, countries can build bridges and strengthen diplomatic ties. This chapter explores the significance of cultural diplomacy and its impact on global progress.

Cultural diplomacy involves the exchange of ideas, values, traditions, and artistic expressions between countries. It is a powerful tool for soft power, allowing nations to influence and engage with foreign publics in a non-coercive manner. Through cultural diplomacy, countries can showcase their cultural heritage, promote their values, and create a positive image on the global stage. This fosters goodwill and enhances diplomatic relations, paving the way for cooperation in various fields, including trade, security, and development.

One of the key benefits of cultural diplomacy is its ability to break down stereotypes and misconceptions. By exposing individuals to different cultures and perspectives, cultural exchange programs promote mutual understanding and empathy. For example, international student exchange programs enable young people to immerse themselves in different cultural contexts, broadening their horizons and fostering cross-cultural friendships. Similarly, cultural festivals and exhibitions provide platforms for showcasing diverse artistic traditions, celebrating shared humanity, and promoting dialogue.

Moreover, cultural diplomacy can contribute to conflict resolution and peacebuilding. In regions affected by political tensions or conflicts, cultural initiatives can serve as bridges for dialogue and reconciliation. Art, music, and literature have the power to transcend political divides and touch the hearts of people, creating spaces for healing and understanding. For instance, cultural exchange projects in post-conflict societies have facilitated reconciliation by bringing together individuals from different communities and promoting dialogue through creative expressions.

In the context of globalization, cultural diplomacy also plays a role in promoting cultural diversity and safeguarding cultural heritage. As global interconnectedness increases, there is a risk of cultural homogenization and the erosion of local traditions. Cultural diplomacy initiatives help preserve and celebrate cultural diversity by supporting the transmission of cultural knowledge and practices. This not only enriches global cultural heritage but also empowers communities to take pride in their cultural identities.

Chapter 6: The Influence of Technology on Global Culture Technology has revolutionized the way we live, work, and connect with one another, profoundly impacting global culture. From the internet to social media, technological advancements have transformed communication, information sharing, and cultural expression. This chapter explores the influence of technology on global culture and its implications for progress.

The internet has democratized access to information, enabling people from all corners of the globe to connect and share knowledge. This has led to the emergence of a global information society, where ideas and cultural content can be disseminated rapidly and widely. Online platforms like Wikipedia, YouTube, and social media have become key repositories of collective knowledge and creativity. This digital exchange fosters a sense of global community and empowers individuals to contribute to and benefit from shared cultural resources.

Social media, in particular, has transformed the way people communicate and engage with culture. Platforms like Instagram, TikTok, and Twitter allow individuals to share their experiences, opinions, and creative works with a global audience. This has given rise to new forms of cultural expression, such as memes, viral videos, and online art movements. Social media influencers and content creators have become cultural icons, shaping trends and influencing public discourse. This digital culture is characterized by its immediacy, interactivity, and participatory nature.

However, the influence of technology on global culture is not without challenges. The digital divide remains a significant issue, with unequal access to technology and the internet across different regions and socio-economic groups. This can exacerbate existing inequalities and limit the participation of marginalized communities in the digital cultural landscape. Additionally, the spread of misinformation and digital echo chambers can distort cultural narratives and polarize societies. Addressing these challenges requires concerted efforts to promote digital literacy, bridge the digital divide, and foster inclusive and responsible online communities.

Moreover, the rapid pace of technological change raises questions about cultural preservation and sustainability. As digital platforms evolve and new technologies emerge, there is a risk of losing valuable cultural content that is not adequately archived or maintained. Efforts to digitize and preserve cultural heritage must be prioritized to ensure that future generations can access and appreciate the richness of global cultural diversity. By embracing the potential of technology while addressing its challenges, societies can harness its power to enhance cultural exchange, creativity, and progress.

Chapter 7: Global Trade and Economic Development Global trade has been a driving force behind economic development, lifting millions of people out of poverty and fostering prosperity around the world. By opening markets and facilitating the exchange of goods, services, and ideas, global trade promotes economic growth and innovation. This chapter explores the benefits and challenges of global trade and its impact on economic development.

One of the primary benefits of global trade is the efficient allocation of resources. By specializing in the production of goods and services in which they have a comparative advantage, countries can maximize their productivity and trade with others to meet their needs. This specialization and exchange lead to increased economic output and higher living standards. For example, countries with abundant natural resources can export them to countries that lack them, while importing advanced technologies and manufactured goods in return. This mutually beneficial trade fosters economic interdependence and cooperation.

Global trade also drives innovation and technological advancement. Exposure to international markets encourages businesses to adopt best practices, improve their products, and invest in research and development. Competition from foreign firms can spur domestic companies to innovate and enhance their competitiveness. Additionally, the exchange of ideas and technologies across borders facilitates the diffusion of knowledge and innovation. This dynamic process contributes to the development of new industries and the creation of high-quality jobs, boosting economic growth.

However, global trade is not without its challenges. Trade liberalization can lead to economic dislocation and job losses in certain sectors, particularly in industries that face competition from cheaper imports. Workers in these sectors may experience wage stagnation or unemployment, leading to social and economic inequalities. To address these challenges, governments must implement policies that support workers in transitioning to new industries and acquiring new skills. Trade adjustment assistance programs, investment in education and training, and social safety nets are essential to ensure that the benefits of global trade are widely shared.

Moreover, global trade can have environmental impacts, as the production and transportation of goods contribute to carbon emissions and resource depletion. Sustainable trade practices, such as green technologies, eco-friendly supply chains, and international environmental agreements, are crucial to mitigating these impacts. By balancing economic growth with environmental sustainability, global trade can contribute to long-term prosperity and well-being.

Chapter 8: The Power of Multinational Corporations Multinational corporations (MNCs) wield significant influence in the global economy, shaping markets, driving innovation, and impacting societies. With their vast resources and extensive reach, MNCs have the potential to be powerful agents of change. This chapter examines the role of multinational corporations in global progress and the responsibilities they bear.

One of the primary strengths of multinational corporations is their ability to mobilize resources on a large scale. By operating across multiple countries, MNCs can leverage economies of scale, access diverse markets, and allocate resources efficiently. This enables them to invest in cutting-edge technologies, research and development, and large-scale infrastructure projects. For example, MNCs in the pharmaceutical industry have the capacity to conduct extensive research, develop new treatments, and distribute life-saving medications globally. Their contributions to innovation and public health are substantial.

In addition to their economic impact, multinational corporations play a crucial role in fostering international collaboration and cultural exchange. By employing diverse workforces and engaging with local communities, MNCs create opportunities for cross-cultural interactions and knowledge transfer. This cultural diversity enhances creativity, problem-solving, and adaptability within organizations. Furthermore, MNCs can act as bridges between different markets and regions, facilitating the flow of goods, services, and ideas. This interconnectedness contributes to a more integrated and cooperative global economy.

However, the influence of multinational corporations also raises important ethical and social considerations. MNCs must navigate complex regulatory environments, labor practices, and environmental standards in the countries where they operate. Instances of labor exploitation, environmental degradation, and tax avoidance have raised concerns about the accountability and ethical conduct of some MNCs. To address these challenges, multinational corporations must adopt responsible business practices, adhere to international standards, and engage in transparent and accountable governance.

Moreover, MNCs have a responsibility to contribute to the social and economic development of the communities in which they operate. This includes creating quality jobs, investing in local infrastructure, and supporting education and healthcare initiatives. Corporate social responsibility (CSR) programs are essential for ensuring that the benefits of MNC operations are shared with local communities. By aligning their business strategies with social and environmental goals, multinational corporations can contribute to sustainable development and global progress.

Chapter 9: The Role of International Organizations in Global Progress International organizations play a vital role in addressing global challenges and promoting progress through cooperation and collaboration. By bringing together countries and stakeholders from around the world, these organizations facilitate dialogue, coordinate efforts, and implement policies that address issues such as poverty, health, and environmental sustainability. This chapter explores the contributions of international organizations to global progress and the challenges they face.

One of the key functions of international organizations is to provide a platform for dialogue and negotiation. Organizations like the United Nations (UN), the World Trade Organization (WTO), and the World Health Organization (WHO) enable countries to come together to discuss and address global issues. Through diplomatic negotiations, international agreements, and multilateral treaties, these organizations promote peace, stability, and cooperation. For example, the Paris Agreement, facilitated by the UN, represents a collective effort to combat climate change and reduce greenhouse gas emissions on a global scale.

International organizations also play a critical role in providing technical assistance and capacity-building support to developing countries. By offering expertise, funding, and resources, organizations like the World Bank, the International Monetary Fund (IMF), and the United Nations Development Programme (UNDP) help countries implement development projects and improve their socio-economic conditions. These initiatives focus on areas such as education, healthcare, infrastructure, and governance, contributing to poverty reduction and sustainable development.

Moreover, international organizations are instrumental in coordinating responses to global crises and emergencies. During natural disasters, pandemics, and conflicts, organizations like the WHO, the International Red Cross, and the United Nations High Commissioner for Refugees (UNHCR) provide humanitarian aid, medical assistance, and support for displaced populations. Their efforts are crucial in saving lives, alleviating suffering, and rebuilding communities in the aftermath of crises.

However, international organizations face challenges in navigating complex geopolitical dynamics, securing funding, and ensuring effective implementation of their programs. Political tensions, competing interests, and limited resources can hinder their ability to achieve their mandates. Strengthening the capacity and effectiveness of international organizations requires sustained commitment from member states, adequate funding, and robust governance structures. By fostering inclusive and transparent decision-making processes, international organizations can enhance their impact and contribute to global progress.

Chapter 10: The Future of Global Governance Global governance is evolving in response to the complex and interconnected challenges of the 21st century. As issues such as climate change, cybersecurity, and global health transcend national borders, there is a growing need for innovative and collaborative approaches to governance. This chapter explores the future of global governance and the principles that will guide its development.

One of the key principles of future global governance is inclusivity. Effective governance requires the participation of diverse stakeholders, including governments, international organizations, civil society, the private sector, and local communities. Inclusive governance ensures that the voices and perspectives of all stakeholders are considered in decision-making processes. This fosters greater legitimacy, accountability, and resilience in addressing global challenges. For example, the involvement of indigenous communities in climate change negotiations has led to more comprehensive and culturally sensitive approaches to environmental protection.

Another principle is adaptability. The rapidly changing global landscape demands flexible and responsive governance structures that can adapt to new challenges and opportunities. This includes leveraging technology and data to inform decision-making, monitoring progress, and adjusting strategies as needed. Digital governance platforms, data analytics, and artificial intelligence can enhance the efficiency and effectiveness of global governance. By embracing innovation and continuous learning, global governance systems can remain relevant and impactful.

Furthermore, future global governance must prioritize sustainability. Addressing the long-term health of our planet and societies requires integrating sustainable development goals (SDGs) into governance frameworks. This involves balancing economic growth with environmental protection, social equity, and balancing economic growth with environmental protection, social equity, and sustainable resource management. Future governance must also prioritize the well-being of people and the planet, ensuring that development is inclusive and respects the ecological boundaries of our world.

Chapter 11: Global Health and Development The health of populations is a crucial determinant of global progress and development. Access to quality healthcare, disease prevention, and public health infrastructure are essential for improving the well-being of individuals and communities. This chapter explores the relationship between global health and development, highlighting key challenges and opportunities for progress.

One of the primary challenges in global health is the disparity in access to healthcare services. While some countries have advanced healthcare systems, others struggle with limited resources, inadequate infrastructure, and a shortage of healthcare professionals. These disparities result in significant health inequalities, with vulnerable populations bearing the brunt of preventable diseases and poor health outcomes. Addressing this challenge requires a concerted effort to strengthen health systems, invest in healthcare infrastructure, and ensure equitable access to essential services for all.

Preventive healthcare and public health initiatives play a vital role in promoting global health. Vaccination programs, disease surveillance, and health education campaigns are effective strategies for preventing the spread of infectious diseases and improving population health. For example, the global effort to eradicate polio has made significant progress, reducing the incidence of the disease by more than 99% since the 1980s. Similarly, initiatives to combat HIV/AIDS, tuberculosis, and malaria have saved millions of lives and contributed to overall health improvement.

Another critical aspect of global health is addressing the social determinants of health, such as education, income, and living conditions. Health outcomes are closely linked to these socio-economic factors, and efforts to improve health must be integrated with broader development initiatives. For instance, improving access to clean water and sanitation, enhancing educational opportunities, and reducing poverty can have a profound impact on health and well-being. By addressing the root causes of health disparities, societies can achieve more sustainable and equitable development.

Innovation and technology are also driving advancements in global health. Telemedicine, mobile health applications, and digital health platforms are transforming the delivery of healthcare services, especially in remote and underserved areas. These technologies enable healthcare providers to reach patients, monitor health conditions, and deliver timely interventions. Additionally, advancements in medical research and biotechnology are leading to new treatments, vaccines, and diagnostic tools. By harnessing the power of innovation, the global health community can overcome challenges and achieve significant progress in health and development.

Chapter 12: The Future of Global Progress As we look to the future, it is clear that global progress will be shaped by the interplay of politics, culture, and business. The challenges and opportunities of the 21st century demand innovative and collaborative approaches to address complex issues and drive sustainable development. This chapter explores the vision for the future of global progress and the principles that will guide us forward.

One of the guiding principles for future progress is sustainability. Ensuring that development meets the needs of the present without compromising the ability of future generations to meet their own needs is paramount. This involves adopting sustainable practices in all aspects of life, from business operations to daily living. By prioritizing sustainability, we can protect the environment, preserve natural resources, and promote the well-being of people and the planet.

Another important principle is inclusivity. Global progress must be inclusive, ensuring that all individuals and communities have the opportunity to benefit from development. This includes addressing inequalities, promoting social justice, and empowering marginalized groups. Inclusive development fosters social cohesion, reduces disparities, and creates a more equitable and just world. By embracing diversity and promoting equal opportunities, we can build a future where everyone can thrive.

Collaboration and partnership are also essential for future progress. The interconnected nature of global challenges requires coordinated efforts and collective action. Governments, businesses, international organizations, civil society, and individuals must work together to achieve common goals. By leveraging the strengths and resources of different stakeholders, we can amplify our impact and drive meaningful change. Collaboration fosters innovation, knowledge sharing, and mutual support, enabling us to tackle complex issues more effectively.

Finally, resilience and adaptability are crucial for navigating the uncertainties of the future. The world is constantly evolving, and we must be prepared to respond to new challenges and seize emerging opportunities. Building resilient systems and communities involves enhancing our capacity to withstand shocks, recover from disruptions, and adapt to changing circumstances. By fostering resilience and embracing adaptability, we can create a future that is not only prosperous but also resilient to the uncertainties of the 21st century.

In conclusion, the future of global progress is shaped by the dynamic interplay of politics, culture, and business. By embracing principles of sustainability, inclusivity, collaboration, and resilience, we can navigate the complexities of the modern world and drive meaningful change. As we move forward, it is essential to recognize the interconnectedness of our global community and work together to build a more just, equitable, and sustainable future for all.

2

Chapter 13: The Role of Education in Global Progress

Education is a cornerstone of global progress, empowering individuals and communities to improve their lives and contribute to societal development. Access to quality education fosters critical thinking, creativity, and problem-solving skills, which are essential for addressing complex global challenges. This chapter explores the impact of education on global progress and the strategies for promoting inclusive and equitable education.

Education is a powerful tool for social and economic mobility. It equips individuals with the knowledge and skills needed to secure better job opportunities, increase their earning potential, and improve their quality of life. Access to education also promotes gender equality, as it empowers women and girls to participate fully in economic, political, and social life. Educated women are more likely to make informed decisions about their health, have fewer children, and invest in the education of their children, creating a positive cycle of development.

Moreover, education fosters social cohesion and civic engagement. Schools and universities provide spaces for diverse individuals to interact, share ideas, and develop mutual understanding and respect. Education also encourages active citizenship, as it equips individuals with the knowledge and skills needed to participate in democratic processes, advocate for their rights, and contribute to their communities. By promoting inclusive and equitable education, societies can build stronger, more cohesive communities.

However, many challenges remain in ensuring access to quality education for all. Disparities in education access and quality persist, particularly in low-income and rural areas. Factors such as poverty, conflict, and discrimination can limit educational opportunities for marginalized groups. Addressing these challenges requires targeted interventions, including investment in education infrastructure, teacher training, and inclusive policies that ensure all individuals, regardless of their background, have the opportunity to learn and succeed.

Innovation and technology play a crucial role in advancing education. Digital learning platforms, online courses, and educational apps have the potential to expand access to quality education, particularly in remote and underserved areas. These technologies enable personalized learning, where students can learn at their own pace and receive targeted support. By harnessing the power of technology, education systems can become more inclusive, adaptable, and resilient, contributing to global progress.

Chapter 14: The Role of Media in Shaping Public Opinion and Global Discourse Media plays a pivotal role in shaping public opinion and influencing global discourse. As a powerful tool for communication and information dissemination, media has the capacity to inform, educate, and mobilize people around important issues. This chapter examines the impact of media on global progress and the responsibilities of media organizations in fostering informed and responsible discourse.

Media serves as a watchdog, holding governments, businesses, and other institutions accountable for their actions. Investigative journalism, for example, exposes corruption, human rights abuses, and environmental violations, prompting public outcry and action. By shining a light on issues that might otherwise remain hidden, media can drive positive change and promote transparency and accountability. Furthermore, media coverage of social movements and advocacy campaigns can amplify marginalized voices and bring attention to issues of social justice and inequality.

Media also plays a critical role in shaping public perceptions and attitudes. News coverage, documentaries, and opinion pieces can influence how people understand and respond to global challenges such as climate change, migration, and public health. Media can frame issues in ways that either promote or hinder progress. For example, responsible reporting on climate change can raise awareness and motivate action, while sensationalist or biased coverage can perpetuate misinformation and apathy. Media organizations have a responsibility to provide accurate, balanced, and ethical reporting that fosters informed and constructive public discourse.

However, the media landscape is also fraught with challenges. The rise of digital and social media has democratized information dissemination but has also led to the spread of misinformation, fake news, and echo chambers. These phenomena can distort public understanding and polarize societies. Addressing these challenges requires a multi-faceted approach, including media literacy education, fact-checking initiatives, and regulatory frameworks that promote responsible journalism and combat misinformation.

Moreover, media organizations must navigate the tension between commercial interests and public service. The pursuit of profits can sometimes lead to sensationalism and superficial coverage, undermining the media's role in fostering informed and critical public discourse. To uphold their responsibilities, media organizations must prioritize ethical journalism, invest in investigative reporting, and engage with diverse perspectives. By doing so, media can contribute to a more informed, engaged, and empowered global citizenry.

Chapter 15: The Impact of Migration on Global Progress Migration has been a driving force behind human progress for centuries, shaping the cultural, economic, and social landscapes of societies around the world. As people move in search of better opportunities, they bring with them skills, knowledge, and cultural diversity that enrich host communities. This chapter explores the impact of migration on global progress and the challenges and opportunities it presents.

Migration contributes to economic development by filling labor shortages, driving innovation, and increasing productivity. Migrants often take on jobs that are in high demand but may be less attractive to local workers, such as those in agriculture, construction, and healthcare. Their contributions help sustain key sectors of the economy and support the provision of essential services. Moreover, highly skilled migrants bring expertise and innovation, fostering technological advancement and economic growth. Countries that embrace and integrate migrants can benefit from their talents and drive.

Cultural exchange is another significant impact of migration. As people from different backgrounds interact, they share their traditions, languages, and ways of life, leading to vibrant and diverse societies. This cultural diversity enhances creativity, broadens perspectives, and fosters mutual understanding and respect. For example, multicultural cities often become hubs of artistic and intellectual activity, attracting tourists, investors, and talent from around the world. Migration enriches the cultural fabric of societies and promotes global interconnectedness.

However, migration also poses challenges that need to be addressed. Integrating migrants into host communities requires careful planning and support to ensure social cohesion and prevent discrimination. Migrants may face barriers such as language differences, legal restrictions, and social exclusion. Policies that promote inclusive and equitable integration are essential for harnessing the benefits of migration and ensuring that all individuals can contribute to and benefit from progress.

Additionally, migration can have mixed effects on countries of origin. While remittances from migrants provide significant financial support to families and communities, the emigration of skilled workers, known as brain drain, can deplete human capital and hinder development. To address this, strategies such as promoting circular migration, where migrants return home with new skills and knowledge, and investing in education and job opportunities in countries of origin, can mitigate the negative impacts and maximize the benefits of migration.

In conclusion, migration is a powerful force that shapes global progress in multifaceted ways. By embracing the opportunities it presents and addressing the challenges it poses, societies can create inclusive, dynamic, and prosperous communities that thrive on diversity and interconnectedness. Migration, when managed effectively, can be a catalyst for global development and progress.

Beyond Maps: How Politics, Culture, and Business Redefine Global Progress

In today's interconnected world, the lines that once defined national boundaries are increasingly blurred. "Beyond Borders" delves into the complex interplay between politics, culture, and business that is reshaping global progress. This book explores how political decisions influence cultural identities and economic landscapes, how cultural diplomacy fosters international relations, and how businesses drive social change. Through twelve insightful chapters, readers will journey through the impacts of technology on global culture, the role of education in fostering development, and the significance of international organizations in addressing global challenges. Each chapter provides a nuanced understanding of how these forces converge to shape our modern world. Join us as we navigate the dynamic intersections of politics, culture, and business, and uncover the pathways to a more inclusive, innovative, and sustainable future.

www.ingramcontent.com/pod-product-compliance
Lightning Source LLC
LaVergne TN
LVHW020508080526
838202LV00057B/6245